46 Days of Christmas

46 DAYS OF CHRISTMAS

A Cycle of Old World Songs,
Legends and Customs

by **DOROTHY GLADYS SPICER**

illustrated by
ANNE MARIE JAUSS

COWARD-McCANN, INC.   NEW YORK

To
K. T.
who makes
victory from defeat

With this book the author pays tribute to Vassar College on the occasion of its centennial.

Some material in *46 Days of Christmas* is adapted from an earlier book, *Festivals of Western Europe* (published by The H. W. Wilson Company) and is used by courtesy of the publisher.

The English version of the Saint Lucia song is by Holger Lundbergh, and is given with the author's permission.

I wish especially to thank Joaquim G. de Vasconcellos for his help in translating the Portuguese songs.

© 1960 by Dorothy Gladys Spicer

Library of Congress Catalog Card Number: 60-12497

MANUFACTURED IN THE UNITED STATES OF AMERICA

Fifth Impression

CONTENTS

INDEXES

PREFACE

In most countries Christmas starts earlier and lasts longer than in the United States. All in all, it takes at least forty-six days to celebrate the holiday properly. *46 Days of Christmas* brings together a few of the many folk poems and hymns of devotion from nineteen countries where the Birthday of Jesus is a feast of long and multiple observances.

In places where life is leisurely and tradition strong, Christmas is a season to savor. To enjoy it completely one must not hurry. One must cherish Christmas as a Dutch child cherishes his Saint Nicholas Eve gingerbread. To eat greedily means loss of flavor. To nibble slowly, share with playmates, and lay some aside for another day, is to relish to the full this once-a-year treat.

In the nineteen-hundred-odd years since Three Kings laid their gifts at the feet of the Child, Christmas has been the great day of remembrance. In most European countries gift-giving belongs to other times. Christmas is a holy season. Christmas means Midnight Mass and lighted tapers. It means a *crèche* under a tree with homemade ornaments, and a family supper with traditional foods. Most of all, Christmas means the carols and hymns, the prayers and verses, that generations of Christians have offered to Jesus.

For years I have been gathering these old folk poems. They are shining beads on the golden thread of Christmas. Each bead tells a story or recalls a memory of the forty-six days — in Italy, Bulgaria, Syria, or France.

I have gleaned material from different sources. Much comes from the memories of men and women who long ago emigrated from the Old World to the New. Poets, priests, and peasants of many faiths and nationalities have generously shared their lore. I found other material in the countries where I have lived and worked. A few selections appear just as they come from the past.

The simplicity and freshness of the original verses have been tenderly guarded in translating and adapting from primary sources. In paraphrasing into English, I have tried to keep the flavor of sound and sense rather than literal meanings. These folk verses and devotional poems have a spirit that survives translation.

Since much of the book is from word-of-mouth tradition, it was sometimes difficult to evaluate material. Folklore is fluid. Folk customs and beliefs vary from person to person and village to village. The same stories appear, of course, in other versions — some of them contradictory — which merely indicates their wide appeal and adaptation.

I hope that *46 Days of Christmas* may give young people a warmer feeling toward the world's Christmas poems and customs. In their variation they offer a deep understanding of the Feast, and the forty-six days in fact are not the limit. The season is really longer.

I have arranged *46 Days of Christmas* in chronological order. This gives a picture of the holiday cycle in countries where Christmas lasts for weeks, instead of days. The index by country is for readers who wish to refer to selections of a given nationality. The index of titles, and one by special days, are additional aids to study.

DOROTHY GLADYS SPICER

December 4
Saint Barbara's Day in Syria

Blessed Saint Barbara

Blessed Saint Barbara,
Thou chosen of God,
Thy stern heathen father, adorer of stone,
Determined to kill thee,
But God was thy Shield.
Thy father's sharp sword,
When he tried to behead thee,
Turned to a necklace of coins most rare;
The rope used to hang thee
Became a silk girdle,
And the fire to burn thee
As sweet incense ascended.
Blessed Saint Barbara,
Thou chosen of God.

Christian children of Syria and Lebanon start Christmas on December 4, the anniversary of Saint Barbara, who was martyred about 235. For centuries girls of many countries have loved and honored the virgin martyr, who became one of the most popular saints of the Middle Ages.

Legend says that Barbara had many suitors. She refused them all because they were pagan, she a Christian. Barbara's stubbornness so angered her father, the rich pagan Dioscorus, that he tried several times to kill her. Each time — as the song suggests — a miracle saved the young girl from harm. Then Dioscorus locked Barbara in a high tower, where no man could see her beauty.

Finally, the authorities denounced Barbara as a Christian and threw her into prison. When the pagan judge condemned her to death, her own father slew her.

In spite of her suffering, the youthful martyr never wavered in her love toward God. This is why Syrian children like Saint Barbara, and their parents teach them of her courage and devotion.

Saint Barbara's Feast means candles of many colors, rich pastries, and candies. Someone always plays the part of the saint in her long white robe and gleaming crown. To Syrians, the Saint Barbara celebration is similar to the American Christmas party. Instead of trimming a tree behind closed doors, the parents secretly decorate a table with lighted candles and with wheat-flour cakes, rich with nuts, sugar, and honey. The wheat is significant, because it commemorates the dead, and symbolizes the immortality of the soul.

When everything is ready, the children gather excitedly outside the party room doors. Saint Barbara, usually impersonated by a favorite aunt or close family friend, waits with the group. When at last the door opens, she leads the children in a procession around the table, all chanting the festival song.

The feast is a merry one, with good things to eat, singing, and masquerading. But Saint Barbara's Day is the time for sharing as well as receiving. Parents send their children with goodies and sweets to the homes of the poor and unfortunate. As the boys and girls present their offerings, they give the traditional greeting: "May God bless you and bring you happiness throughout the year. Father and Mother beg you to accept these gifts from us."

In some places, boys with grotesque masks and raggle-taggle garments visit from door to door in the neighborhood. At each house they demand a "blessing" — meaning candles, money, or candies. The beggars acknowledge their thanks with foolish antics and songs.

11

December 5
Saint Nicholas' Eve in the Netherlands

Saint Nicholas, Good Holy Man

Saint Nicholas, good holy man,
Put on your best cassock.
Ride in it to Amsterdam,
To Amsterdam from Spain.

In the Netherlands, December 5 is Saint Nicholas, or Santa Klaus Eve. For over six hundred years, Saint Nicholas and his Moorish servant, *Zwarte Piet,* or Black Peter, have been bringing Dutch children their holiday gifts.

In Dutch tradition, Saint Nicholas, the fourth-century Bishop of Myra, was born in Spain. The long-bearded bishop wears a white robe, crimson cassock, and tall red miter, or official headdress. In his white-gloved hands he carries a gold-colored crozier, shaped like a shepherd's crook. Each year he and Black Peter journey to Amsterdam from Spain. This part of the legend possibly dates from the sixteenth century, when the Netherlands was under Spanish control.

Usually the saint makes his trip aboard the steamer *Spain.* His retinue follow in the *Madrid.* The boats arrive at the quay amid the clatter of ringing bells, gun salutes, and the shouts of thousands of boys and girls. When Saint Nicholas lands, he mounts a white horse and rides through the streets in a triumphal procession, with the burgomaster and other city officials in attendance. The saint always has so much to do that a whole brigade of Black Peters accompany him on foot, bicycle, or astride little motor scooters that puff, blow and make explosive noises. The saint and his helpers have a busy day since they always visit and leave presents at all city hospitals, schools, and institutions.

In cities throughout the Netherlands the civic welcome to Saint Nicholas is impressive. In recent years the good bishop has even arrived at the Hague by helicopter. But in small towns and villages he traditionally holds to old-fashioned ways and rides over the housetops on his white horse. He jumps from roof to roof with Black Peter at his side. The Moor, who dresses like a medieval page, wears a plumed hat, black doublet and hose, and black gloves.

Naughty children fear Peter, for he carries a yawning black bag. In it are gifts for the good and switches for the bad. If youngsters are *really* bad, he may stuff them into the bag and take them back to Spain. He will not return them to their parents until the following year, when they are more docile and polite.

Early in the evening Saint Nicholas and the Moor appear at every door in the village. In many places December 5 is still called Strewing Eve because, shortly before the visitors arrive, Black Peter supposedly throws *pepernoten,* or hard round spice cakes, down the chimney. Actually, a bell rings loudly and the door opens a crack. Then a black-gloved hand appears and strews a handful of peppernuts across the floor. As the children scramble for the cakes they greet Saint Nicholas with little songs. Although the rhymes vary from place to place, the simple four-line verse to "Saint Nicholas, good holy man" is a traditional favorite. After the singing, the saint appears and questions Mientje, Hans, and little Lies about their behavior during the past year.

Later the same night while the youngsters sleep, Saint Nicholas and Black Peter make their rooftop visits. Peter slips down the chimney, for the saint must not soil his fine robes with soot. The Moor puts presents in the wooden shoes which the children have set in a row near the chimney. But first he removes the offerings the boys and girls leave for the saint's white horse. There may be lump sugar or pumpernickel — sometimes only a carrot, a wisp of hay, or a cup of water. Each child gives according to his means.

Among the presents Black Peter leaves are pink and white

candy hearts, with creamy filling; spiced honey gingerbreads, cut into human and animal shapes; and often immense gingerbread figures of Saint Nicholas on his horse, or Black Peter with his bag. Everyone envies the recipients of such cakes because they last for days. Of course, there are colored marzipans shaped like apples, potatoes, and fat little pigs.

Black Peter often leaves switches along with the sweets, to remind children to behave. When his work at a house is finished, the Moor climbs back up the chimney and rejoins Saint Nicholas. Together they whisk through the night to the next rooftop.

December 6
Saint Nicholas' Day in Lorraine, France

Saint Nicholas, My Good Patron

Saint Nicholas, my good patron,
Send me something nice,
Send me something nice.

Tradition says that the Virgin gave Lorraine to Saint Nicholas as a reward. Naturally the saint, who is guardian of the province, is the special patron of its children, and his feast day, December 6, is a time of unusual gaiety. This does not mean that Saint Nicholas neglects annual visits to other parts of France. It is just that he feels more at home in Lorraine, and his own boys and girls make a great fuss over him. The saint always brings them candies and nuts if they are good.

In various parts of Lorraine, the saint walks through the streets on his anniversary. He makes an imposing figure in his crimson bishop's robes and pointed miter. The children always cheer and clap at the sight of Saint Nicholas, but they shrink back in fear from his inseparable companion, *Père Fouettard.* *Le Père,* like Holland's Zwarte Piet, carries a bundle of switches. He has an uncomfortably long memory, too, and always seems to know which boys and girls were disobedient during the past twelve months. Now and then he playfully smacks some youngster's toes in passing. What guilty children really fear is the possibility of a genuine whipping. Even worse, le Père may advise Saint Nicholas to pass them by when he makes his secret rounds at night.

In some places a fascinating feature of the Saint Nicholas Day procession is a cart with a salt barrel. Sticking out of the top are figures of three naked boys. The group represents one of the saint's most famous miracles. It also explains why Saint Nicholas became the special patron of young boys, although he loves little girls equally well.

Legend says that in the fourth century, when Nicholas was Archbishop of Myra, in Asia Minor, three school boys journeyed through the town. They were sons of an Oriental nobleman who had asked them to call on the holy man. Since it was late when the boys arrived, they decided to spend the night at the tavern and see the Bishop next day.

Soon they fell sound asleep. The innkeeper, thinking of a new way to make a profit, murdered his guests in their sleep. Then he cut up their bodies and salted them down in a keg of brine. He planned to serve the flesh to his customers and save on the cost of meat.

That night Saint Nicholas had a dream. It revealed the horrid crime. He woke, threw on his robes and hurried to the tavern. There he accused the guilty landlord, and brought the three boys back to life. From that day on, Saint Nicholas has been the patron of all children, but especially of schoolboys.

On the saint's eve boys and girls of Lorraine, like those of Holland, place their shoes near the chimney. After singing a few lines to Saint Nicholas, they go to bed. In the morning the shoes overflow with sweetmeats. But since Père Fouettard is always alert to naughtiness, even good children receive ribbon-tied birch twigs, along with gifts from the saint.

December 6
Saint Nicholas' Day in Luxembourg

Good Saint Nicholas

O, good Saint Nicholas, patron of school children,
Bring me bonbons for my little basket.
I want to be good, like a little lamb,
To learn my lessons, so I'll get bonbons.
O, good Saint Nicholas, O, good, O, good Saint Nicholas.

Young people of Luxembourg, as of Holland, France, and other countries, anticipate *Neklosdag,* the Feast of Saint Nicholas, for days, weeks, and months in advance. On the Sunday preceding his festival, the Grand Duchy officially welcomes the saint in towns and villages. In some places, as in Echternach, Saint Nicholas and his companion. *Hoësecker,* make their spectacular arrival by boat. The mayor, in his finest robes, and the aldermen await their distinguished guests at the bank of the river Sûre. The town officials escort their visitors to a horse-drawn carriage, decorated with branches of fir. A procession forms quickly. The local band plays loudly. The carriage begins to bump along the cobbled streets.

In Luxembourg, Saint Nicholas wears a red silk robe and a tall bishop's miter. He has a long gray beard, and his merry eyes twinkle behind rimmed spectacles. In his gloved hands he carries the golden crooked staff that is his badge of office.

A crowd of rosy-cheeked, mittened children surges through the narrow streets. They shout, hop, and jump excitedly as Saint Nicholas and Hoësecker make their triumphal approach to the old Town Hall in the market place. The band plays all the songs the boys and girls know. They, in turn, beg their saint for bonbons in verses addressed to Good Saint Nicholas.

The children dread Hoësecker as much as they love Saint Nicholas. Like Père Fouettard, Hoësecker carries switches on his back and he never hesitates to whip the lazy or disobedient child. But today every child is very good. At the ceremonies in the market place each one receives a big paper bag bulging with apples, cakes, and bonbons. The little ones in their mother's arms get their presents first, then the children up to twelve. Youngsters clutch their bags happily, and in their excitement often spill the contents over the cobblestones. Meanwhile, the band strikes up one lively Christmas tune after another.

Christmas Eve in Luxembourg is a family gathering. The tree, beautiful with wax tapers and colored balls, holds the place of honor in the "best" room. Beneath the evergreen branches is the miniature Nativity with carved wooden figures of Jesus, Joseph and Mary, the shepherds and the Kings. As in other countries, families hand down these nativity characters from one generation to the next, and treasure them from Christmas to Christmas.

Seven in the evening is the time to light the candles on the tree. The family enters the room singing carols. After a cold buffet supper, presents are distributed. Children amuse themselves with games and gifts, and adults with songs and conversation, until time for church.

After Midnight Mass people hurry home for the traditional Christmas supper of black pudding and roasted sausages, with white cabbage, boiled potatoes, and wine or beer to drink.

December 13
Saint Lucia's Day in Sweden

Saint Lucia

Night goes with silent steps
Round house and cottage.
O'er the earth the sun forgot
Dark shadows linger.
Then on the threshold stands
White-clad, in candlelight,
Santa Lucia, Santa Lucia.

This song opens the Swedish Christmas season on December 13, *Luciadagen,* or Saint Lucia's Day. Although the day is primarily a home festival, celebrated by rich and poor in every part of the country, it is also observed officially in factories, offices, and public institutions.

Saint Lucia is always represented by a young girl who wears a white dress and crimson sash and stockings. She has a *lingon,* or whortleberry leaf crown, into which white lighted candles are inserted. She announces Yuletide at dawn by stopping at the bedside of each member of the family with a tray of coffee and cakes. The custom goes back to the legend of Saint Lucia, who was condemned to death in 304 during the reign of the Roman Emperor, Diocletian.

Tradition says that Lucia was born at Syracuse, in Sicily, of a noble Christian family. The young girl had her own eyes removed, because their beauty had attracted a pagan suitor. When Lucia rejected him, he denounced her as a Christian. First her jailers tortured her. Eventually they killed her with a sword.

Lucia has always been loved in southern Europe and especially in her native Sicily. There the devout celebrate her death day with bonfires, fireworks, and torchlight processions. The name Lucia means "light." Since the saint supposedly became

23

blind at the darkest season of the year, people think it fitting
to honor her with many lights.

Early missionaries carried the Lucia story to Sweden. There
the legend of the young martyr took deep root in popular imagination. Santa Lucia of Sicily became the Lucia Bride of Sweden.
Now her day stands for hospitality at home and in the com-
munity. Old people once claimed they could see the Lucia Bride
between three and four, on the morning of December 13. She
wore white robes and a crown of light, as she glided across the
icy lakes and snow-covered hills with food and drink for the
parish poor.

This tradition probably accounts for the modern custom of
the Lucia Bride. In the home the oldest daughter enacts the role.
In some villages one young girl is elected to visit each household with a tray of coffee and cakes. In Stockholm and other
large cities there are many Lucia Brides.

In smaller places Saint Lucia usually makes her rounds alone.
Sometimes groups of young parishioners accompany her. The
boys, who are called Star Boys, wear white costumes and tall
peaked caps decorated with cut-outs of moon and stars. They
always carry a paper star lantern fastened to the end of a long
pole. The star — which is lighted from inside — revolves like
a pinwheel. The girls wear long white dresses. They carry lighted
white tapers. Sometimes baker boys are in the group. They offer
ginger cookies and "Lucy cats," or buns flavored with crushed
cardamon and baked in the shape of a letter X. Originally the
form probably stood for the Greek letter *chi,* which looks like
an X and begins the name of Christ.

Luciadagen is a happy occasion not only because of the traditional refreshments and fun, but because the day supposedly
marks the completion of the busiest holiday chores. Young people have finished their Christmas gifts. The farmer has threshed
and put his barns and storerooms to rights. As for the housewife, she not only has made the tallow dips, scoured the copper,

and scrubbed the floor, but has also started to prepare the *lut-fisk,* or stockfish. This fish, traditional to the Christmas Day dinner and the most important item on the menu, requires a full three weeks of soaking, cleaning, and scrubbing before it is ready to cook.

December 24
Christmas Eve in England

The Storke
A Christmas Ballad

The Storke she rose on Christmas Eve
And sayèd unto her broode,
I nowe muste fare to Bethleem
To viewe the Sonne of God.

She gave to eche his dole of mete,
She stowed them fayrlie in.
And faire she flew and faste she flew
And came to Bethleem.

Now where is He of David's lynne?
She asked at house and halle.
He is not here, they spake hardlye,
But in th maungier stalle.

She found Hym in the maungier stalle
With that most Holye Mayde;
The gentyle Storke she wept to see
The Lord so rudelye layde.

Then from her pantynge brest she plucked
The fethers whyte and warm;
She strawes them in the maungier bed
To kepe the Lord from harm.

"Now blessed bee the gentyle Storke
Forever more," quothe Hee,

"For that she saw my sadde estate
And showèd Pytye.

"Full welkum shall she ever bee,
In hamlet and in halle,
And hight henceforth the Blessed Byrd
And friend of babyes all."

This tender English ballad tells how the stork became the patron of babies. Supposedly the verses were found in 1549, handwritten in Old English on the flyleaf of King Edward VI's Prayer Book. The young monarch — then twelve years old — was the only child of Henry VIII and Jane Seymour. The boy, who was highly intelligent but physically weak, died in 1553 at the age of sixteen. During his brief reign the *Book of Common Prayer* was introduced into the Church of England.

For centuries, the stork — one of the most fascinating and individual of all birds — has been a favorite subject of folk legend and belief. Sometimes, as in this ballad, the bird is able to speak. From early times she has been associated with baby lore. Almost every country has the saying that "the stork brings babies."

It is not surprising that a bird of such handsome appearance and odd habits should excite popular imagination. The stork is an occasional summer visitor to Great Britain and a frequent one along the Rhine valley, in Holland, Denmark, Poland, and many other countries. She prefers to build her big nests on roofs and chimney pots rather than in trees. The dignified bird is more than three feet tall. Often she stands motionless for hours on one red leg or wades across damp pastures with comic gravity. There are different kinds of storks, but the species that is probably most familiar has glossy black and white feathers and a long red bill. The bird patiently bides her time until she spies some unwary frog or insect. Then she moves with incredible speed. Snapping the choice morsel in a powerful pincerlike beak, the stork flies swiftly to her hungry noisy brood in a roof-top nest.

In parts of Germany there is an old folk belief that storks discover unborn babies in springs or brooks. Sometimes the birds find infants in dark mountain caverns; often they get babies from beneath "stork stones." Boys and girls found in this way are "stork children." In some places it is said that an infant will soon arrive if a stork even flies over a house.

Aside from these superstitions regarding babies, all Europeans welcome the stork and claim that her presence brings good luck to the houses where she builds her nest.

December 24 and January 5
Christmas Eve and Epiphany Eve in Syria

Light of Wisdom

Thy nativity, O Jesus,
Came to the world
As the Light of Wisdom.
For at Thy birth
They who worshiped the stars
By a Star were taught to worship Thee,
The Sun of Righteousness,
And to know Thee,
The Orient on High.
Glory to Thee, O Lord.

This stately hymn, chanted at midnight mass, expresses the spirit of the Syrian Christmas. The hymn speaks of the Kings of the East, who came to Bethlehem to seek the Infant Jesus. These Wise Men belonged to a class of priests who devoted their lives to the study of the stars and other natural phenomena. As we learn in the Gospel story, the Christmas star guided the Magi from their own country — probably Chaldea or Persia — to the stable at Bethlehem where Jesus was born.

The biblical story of the Wise Men and the mysterious star is a lively source of folk legend and tradition. This is only natural in a country where Moslems and Christians of different sects have lived side by side for hundreds of years. Almost 14 per cent of Syria's population is Christian; the rest is mainly Moslem. Lebanon — which with Syria was formerly under French mandate — has a population that is 54 per cent Christian, 44 per cent Moslem. Both Syria and Lebanon have many superstitions about *Lilat-al-kadr,* the Night of Destiny, as they call January 5, Epiphany Eve.

There has always been a good deal of discussion about *Lilat-*

al-kadr. The Roman Church declares it is the time when the Magi brought gifts to Jesus. The Greek Church insists it is the anniversary of His baptism. Christians and Moslems alike agree to the legend that at midnight on this eve the trees miraculously bow. Christian Syrians say the trees bent before the Kings after they had worshiped Jesus and so showed them how to go home "the other way." God had warned the Magi in a dream "that they should not return to Herod," who was in Jerusalem, and wished to destroy the Child.

Moslems have another explanation: *Al Koran,* their sacred Scriptures, came from Heaven on the Night of Destiny, and so all trees and, according to some, all animals, bow in honor of the Revelation.

Many children of the Mount Lebanon area believe that the Magic Mule brings blessings and gifts on Epiphany Eve. How the mule became a gift-bearer is explained by this story: One Epiphany Eve a man was traveling by muleback through the countryside. At midnight he tied the beast to a tree and went to a nearby village. When he returned, the animal was not in sight. Hearing a braying high above his head, the man looked up and saw his mule struggling among the branches. Then he knew! At midnight the tree had bent in honor of the Christ Child. When the limbs flew back, they had caught the animal and carried it to the top of the tree. Since then, the mule has been a magic creature. Children leave doors open on Epiphany Eve so he can enter with blessings and gifts. He always arrives exactly at twelve. Although boys and girls watch for him and prop their eyelids open to keep awake, they always seem to go to sleep just before the mule arrives.

Farther south where mules are rare, the Camel of Jesus rides across the desert with presents. Legend says this camel was the youngest of the three to take the Wise Men to Bethlehem. The animal was so exhausted by the long journey, that it lay down and moaned outside the stable door. When Jesus heard its cries,

He lifted his tiny hand and blessed the animal with happiness and immortality. This is the reason why some children sing to the camel at Epiphany and ask him to bring presents to them, just as he once took gifts to Jesus. They always leave a dish of water and a bowl of wheat for the camel. The beast loves good boys and girls and leaves them trinkets and sweets. If they are naughty they find black marks on their wrists when they wake.

In many parts of southern Syria people place candles in their windows on Epiphany Eve. These lights guide the steps of the Christ Child as He journeys across the Judean hills.

Magic mules and bowing trees, the Camel of Jesus, the Child Himself — these are only a few of many miracles of the Night of Destiny, in Syria, where Christ was born.

December 24
Christmas Eve in the Netherlands

A Lovely Child

A lovely Child
Is born to us
Of a Virgin pure.
God comforts us poor people:
For had this Child not been born
We should all be lost.
He belongs to all of us.
O, sweet Lord Jesus,
Because you came for all of us
God saves us all from sin.

This Christmas carol, which is about five hundred years old, belongs to Oldenzaal and no other place in the Netherlands. Oldenzaal, a small manufacturing town in the province of Overijssel, is noted for its fine Christmas music as well as its commercial activities. Throughout Christmas, the townsfolk observe the custom of *midwinterhoorn blazen,* or blowing the midwinter horn from the four corners of the medieval church tower. The champion horn blower of the district selects by competition the best horn blowers from fourteen parishes.

The midwinter horn musicians announce the arrival of Advent at five on the morning of Advent Eve. They give a similar performance each morning until January 6, Three Kings' Day, when Christmas in Holland officially ends. The horn players' composition is unique. Each musician sounds just one note on his horn at one time. When the first note stops, the second begins. When the second note stops, the third begins, and so on, until the entire melody is played.

The winter horn measures about forty-five inches in length.

Usually it is cut from sections of birchwood. When screwed together they form a long, graceful horn. The mouthpiece is made of elder. After the crude horn has been thoroughly soaked in water, it produces a shrill monotonous sound that will carry nearly two miles across the level countryside.

Farmers of Danekamp, Ootmarsum, and other communities in the eastern part of the province start to make their winter horns at the beginning of Advent. Usually one man is the acknowledged winter-horn expert. He makes most of the horns in the district.

All through the holidays farmers play their horns at night, over the wells in the farmyard. The frozen surface acts as a sounding board. On dark winter nights when everything is still, the notes of the horns reverberate from all directions across the ice-sheeted meadows and make music that is primitive and wild.

In pre-Christian times people blew horns at midwinter to expel demons and evil spirits. Today the Netherland farmers blow their horns to banish winter darkness, and welcome Jesus, the Light of the World, to the hearts of men.

December 24
Christmas Eve in Poland

My Fairest Treasure

Lullaby, Jesus,
My fairest Treasure.
Lullaby, Jesus,
My love hath no end.
Lullaby, Jesus,
Sweet little Baby,
Mary's arms hold Thee
In love without end.

When the first star appears on Christmas Eve, Polish families gather to end the holiday fast. First, the head of the household breaks an *oplatek,* a thin large round wafer, with each person and exchanges wishes for happiness and health. The priest blesses these wheat-flour wafers, which are peculiar to Christmas. They are baked in cast-iron molds, and stamped with pictures of the Nativity. Friends and relatives often buy oplatki and enclose them in letters to absent relatives and frineds. In rural areas peasants divide the wafers among their cattle, horses, and sheep so that the animals, too, may share the blessings of Christmas.

The *Wilia,* or Christmas Eve supper, is a delightful occasion. The linen feast cloth looks lumpy in spots because a little hay has been tucked under it here and there as a reminder that Jesus was born in a manger. In some homes there is an extra place at the table, for any stranger who may knock at the door.

Supper itself is a wonderful meal. There are thirteen courses, in memory of Christ and the Twelve Apostles. Usually there is almond or beetroot soup served with mushroom patties. There are many kinds of fish, a poppy-seed paste, and for dessert wheat or rice with honey sauce. To end the meal, there are dozens and dozens of small honey or seed cakes and more preserves and confections than one can count.

The Christmas tree usually stands in a room by itself. There are colored candles and decorations of nuts, apples, and all kinds of homemade ornaments. Often the most charming decorations are made from eggshells, blown out at either end and suspended from the branches by threads. Colored paper, wisps of straw, bits of eiderdown, and cleverly applied spots of paint transform the shells into clowns, angels, or birds of paradise. In many places the Good Star from Heaven — impersonated by a woman in white dress and flowing veil — brings presents for the children at the Christmas tree celebration. The little ones are in awe of her companion, the Father Star, who makes them kneel by the tree, say their prayers and sing songs before he will hand out the gifts.

Christmas is a tender, intimate season to all Polish people. Popular imagination pictures Jesus as a Polish baby, whom they rock and spoil and shower with raisins and sweets. When silver cobwebs appear on the hedgerows and meadows, there is a saying that the Virgin Mary spreads out the diapers of little Jesus to dry. At the Shepherds' Mass on Christmas Eve, when the notes of the shepherds' flutes rise clear and strong above the pealing organ, peasants say that the farm animals who saw the manger birth kneel in adoration and receive the power to speak like men.

December 24
Christmas Eve in Provence, France

Burn, Yule Log, Burn

Burn, Yule log, burn!
Joy! Joy!
God gives us joy.
Noël comes! All blessings come!
May God let us see another year;
And if there are no more of us,
May our numbers be no less!

This ancient chant comes from Provence, where Christmas Eve on the old farms means the *Gros Soupa,* or Great Supper, and a cup of new wine to pour on the Yule log. But before supper and "laying the Yule log," everyone goes to Christmas Eve Mass.

In many parts of Provence this service is called the Festival of Shepherds. At Les Baux, Saint Michel-de-Frigolet, and in other sheep-raising areas, shepherds and shepherdesses dress in regional costume and carry a newborn lamb in a procession around the church. They lay the live animal — a symbol of the Lamb of God in its innocence — in a small two-wheeled cart. A ram draws the wagon, which is decorated with flowers and lighted tapers. The procession walks around the church three times to a joyous flute-and-drum accompaniment. At the altar a young shepherd offers the lamb to the priest. Later the shepherds and the congregation take communion.

In Provence, as elsewhere in France, almost every home prepares a *crèche,* or miniature nativity scene. Provençal children regard making the crèche as their particular contribution to the Christmas festival. They are often ingenious in their use of mosses, lichen, small branches, and pebbles to create scenes that resemble the rocky olive-covered hills of their own region. Models of red-tiled village inns and stables filled with hay make a charming background for the brightly colored clay *santons,* or "little saints." Santons belong to Provence. For approximately three hundred years, native craftsmen have handed down from father to son the secret of making these small images of the Holy family, the shepherds, kings, animals, and familiar village characters.

Shortly before Christmas, santons appear at village fairs all over Provence, but especially at the great fairs of Nice and Marseilles. The children complete their nativity scenes except for the figures of the Kings, which they do not add until Epiphany Eve. They decorate the crèches with three candles — usually one red, one white, and one blue — in honor of the Trinity, as well as the tricolor of France.

In olden times peasant families gathered in the kitchen for the Great Supper. First the children lighted the candles in front of the crèche. Then the grandfather, or the oldest member of the family, and the youngest child laid the Yule log. The old man was a symbol of the year that was passing, the child of the year to come. Traditionally the man and the child carried the log unassisted, but really two strong young boys bore the weight that was too heavy for age and infancy. Three times they carried the log around the kitchen. The finest feast-day cloth covered the long table laid for supper. Lighted tapers burned in the old family candlesticks. After the third time around, the bearers rested the log on the irons in the hearth. The family gathered about and bowed their heads.

The grandfather lifted a cup of wine. Three times he poured some of the sparkling liquid on the log, for on the Eve of the Holy Birth everything commemorated the Three. "In the name of the Father, the Son, and the Holy Ghost," the old man said as he emptied the cup. Straightening his shoulders, he chanted the ancient incantation, "Burn, Yule log, burn!"

Quickly faggots were added. As the log began to glow, everyone shouted, "Joy! Joy!" With toasts and congratulations the Great Supper began.

On Christmas Eve most humble Provençals eat roast goose. Turkey stuffed with sausage and black olives or truffles is for the rich. In folk tradition it was the goose's loud cackling that welcomed the Magi to the stable at Bethlehem. Peasants say they show honor to the bird's hospitality when they eat goose at the supper to commemorate Jesus' birth.

Pike or other fish, snails and mullets, celery and chard are all important to the Great Supper. There are thirteen different desserts — probably for Christ and the Twelve Apostles. These delicacies include nougat, figs, dates, pears, hazelnuts, roast chestnuts, apples, raisins, pears, fruit compotes, almond cakes, and *fougasso,* or cakes baked on the hearth.

When the Yule log has burned out, householders collect the ashes and keep them throughout the year. Should cattle fall ill or lightning strike, wells be polluted or disease threaten, a prayer and a bit of the powdered ash supposedly remedies the evil.

On January 5, Eve of the Magi Kings, the children complete the crèche by adding the figures of the Kings, the camels, and their servants. On this night, the Kings traditionally pass through the village streets on their way to Midnight Mass. At the church there is a large crèche where the Magi bow before the Christ Child with gifts. There is aged King Melchior— bent and bearded — with his offering of sweet incense. Gaspard is young and handsome, and he has a present of gold. Balthazar, the black-faced Moor, holds a jar of myrrh.

In the glow of the sunset the Kings pass by. Children run out to the crossroads to welcome the Magi with cakes, their servants with dried fruits, and the camels with hay. Of course, no child has actually seen the Wise Men, for dusk falls swiftly in Provence. Then, too, the winter sun sets early. Also, the nights are often misty at this time of year.

December 24
Christmas Eve in Czechoslovakia

Sleep Well, Little Jesus

Lullaby,
Sleep well, little Jesus.
We shall borrow
A little fur coat
For Thee.
We shall rock Thee
To gentle slumber.
Lullaby,
Sleep well, little Jesus,
Mary's little Son.

In Czechoslovakia, as in Poland, peasants think the Baby Jesus belongs to them. He was surely born in their country, they say. Native artists often represent the Child in a wooden cradle such as any native child might have. Gaily painted hearts, field flowers, and leaves decorate the crib. Infant angels with pink bodies and tiny wings rock the cradle gently. They feed the Baby Jesus cakes and raisins, offer toys and gifts.

In Czechoslovakia, as in most European countries, the children's Christmas begins on December 5, the Eve of Saint Nicholas. On this night Saint Mikuláše, or Nicholas, comes down from heaven on a golden cord. On his back he carries a basket of apples, nuts, and candies. Saint Mikuláše is generous with these gifts — especially when Anicka and Honza are kind and thoughtful and remember their prayers. He also fills their empty stockings with holiday treats.

The day before Christmas is a time of fasting until the first star appears. Then the family sits down to a traditional supper that includes roe soup, fish, a special braided bread, and a holiday cake, rich in almonds and raisins. Grownups say that a child who

does not eat until the evening meal will see the Golden Pig —
but no one has seen him yet.

On Christmas Eve there is always a lighted tree with a Bethlehem, or miniature Nativity scene under the branches. In some
places *Ježíšek,* the little Jesus Christ, visits the children on His
night and leaves them presents.

Czechs call Christmas Eve *Štědrý Večer,* "the very rich night,"
because there are so many gifts and good things to eat. Even the
farm animals enjoy a share of holiday treats, for they receive por-
tions of the Christmas supper. The bees and the fruit trees get
special offerings of food or drink. All that lives and grows on the
farm must share in the meal, to ensure prosperity in the coming
year.

On Christmas Eve young people play fortunetelling games.
One traditional way to tell the future is to float nutshells with
lighted tapers inside on a tub of water. If a shell moves toward
the center of the tub, the owner will go on a trip, but if the
shell stays near the rim, there will be no journey for the next
twelve months. Two shells floating toward each other indicate
a wedding within the year. When they drift apart, there will be
a year's delay.

At twelve o'clock everyone attends the Midnight Mass, or the
Angelic Mass, as it is often called. Christmas Day is a family
holiday when people usually stay quietly at home.

December 24
Christmas Eve in Sweden

46 Days of Christmas

'Tis Yuletide Again

Now 'tis Yuletide again!
Yuletide will last, I think,
'Till Easter.
No, this cannot be,
For between the two
Comes Lent.

This is the song Swedish families sing at the close of the *Julafton,* or Christmas Eve ceremonies, when adults and children join hands and dance around the lighted tree. Yuletide in Sweden, as the song suggests, lasts a long time. Christmas starts on December 13, *Luciadagen,* and continues a full month. The tree is not officially taken down and decorations packed away until *Tjugondag Knut,* Saint Knut's Day, on January 13, the twentieth day after Christmas.

Twentieth day Knut
Driveth Yule out,

is the rhyme older people sing as the younger members of the family dance around the tree for the last time.

Long before Julafton, Christmas presents are neatly wrapped and sealed with red wax. Each gift — whether it is a pair of mittens, a carved toy, or a hand-loomed scarf — must have an individual jingle. These rhymes, which the recipients read aloud when they open their presents, cause great merriment at the Christmas party.

The men of the family cut down the tree in the woods a few days before Christmas, haul it home by sledge, and set it up behind closed doors. The most popular decorations are the straw goats and pigs, the mythological animals of Thor, the Norse thunder god, and Frey, god of the sun. There are polished apples and gingerbread men. Sweden's blue and yellow national flag is proudly placed on top of the tree, while smaller flags decorate the branches. Hand-dipped candles, cookies, and home-made toys of wood and folded paper make the Swedish tree a unique and beautiful family production.

At six o'clock on Christmas Eve family and friends gather around a big kettle of broth on the kitchen stove, to observe the ancient ceremony of "dipping in the kettle." The kitchens are gay with paper garlands and holiday decorations. Lighted candles in three-branched candlesticks symbolize the Trinity, while sweet-smelling straw scattered over the well-scrubbed floor recalls the birth in a stable.

The great kettle with its steaming broth made from sausages, pork, and corned beef fills the kitchen with a tantalizing aroma. Each person spears a piece of dark bread on a fork, dips the slice into the kettle and eats it with a piece of meat. This custom always preceded the Christmas feast "for luck." Except in the country, the meal starts in the kitchen and ends in the dining room. It traditionally includes an enormous array of *smörgåsbord,* or appetizers, and *lutfisk,* the holiday cod that housewives began to prepare on Luciadagen.

After dinner, the Christmas tree is lighted. Before *Jultomten,* the Swedish Santa Claus, arrives, the family sits beside the laden branches and the father reads about the Christ Child's birth. A few old carols follow. Suddenly there is a loud knocking. With whoops of excitement the children race to the door to admit Jultomen, who comes in a sleigh pulled by *Julbokar,* the goats of the ancient thunder god. The role of Jultomten — like that of Santa Claus in the United States — is usually played by an uncle, a big brother, or some other male member of the family. Like Santa, Jultomten has a long white beard and red suit, and carries a sack filled with toys and candies.

Jultomten in this modern guise is fairly recent in Sweden. For hundreds of years he lived on farms as a little gray-bearded gnome in a red suit and peaked red cap. He made his home in the garret, or loft, and kept a sharp eye on everything that happened. He was a temperamental little fellow. Jultomten had to be treated well if the cows were to give milk, the hens to lay, and the crops to prosper. He did not like quarreling or bickering or cheating. He could never endure nasty words. At Yuletide he always had his bowl of rice pudding. Someone placed it in the loft on Christmas Eve. By morning the bowl was as clean as if the old yellow cat, Jultomten's constant friend and companion, had polished it off herself.

Jultomten, the ancient guardian of the farm, will always live in Swedish imagination. You can see his picture on Christmas cards. His red cap is askew and his lips twist in an elfish smile. In one hand he holds a long wooden spoon. He sits cross-legged and content before a huge bowl of Christmas porridge.

December 24
Christmas Eve in Germany

Mary On The Mountain

Upon the mountain
The wind blows wild.
There Mary tends her Child.
She rocks him with her snow-white hand;
No other cradle has she.
"O, Joseph, dear Joseph,
Help me rock my little Child."
"How can I rock the Child for thee?
My numbed fingers scarce will bend."
"Bye-lo, bye-lo, bye."

This traditional cradle-rocking carol is one of many old Christmas songs that feature a dialogue between Mary and Joseph. Sometimes the conversation has a comic twist. Sometimes, as here, the song suggests that Joseph is either an old man with stiff joints or he is numb with cold.

Christmas in Germany is a children's festival. Although Christmas Eve celebrations vary from place to place, families gather everywhere for carols, presents, and a tree with lights, gingerbread animals, red apples, and gilded nuts.

In many places, the holiday excitement starts in November or early December with a holiday fair in the market place. Hamburg's ancient *Dom* is probably one of the most famous fairs, not only in Germany but in the world. The *Christkindlsmarkt,* Kriss Kringle's Fair, in Nuremberg is so old that no one knows when it began.

This fair features Nuremberg's "gold angel." In medieval times people came to the fair from distant places, as they still do. They combined merrymaking, buying, and selling, with going to church. There they saw the priest symbolically "give away the Christ Child" to the children in the form of a doll. After the Reformation, when few remembered the original custom, the Christ Child doll became the Christmas angel. Today a child in gold-colored robes represents the gold angel, and recites verses of welcome to the fair.

Nuremberg's toymakers are busy for months in advance. They make thousands of gold angels to watch over the fair, to decorate the homes, and to dangle from the stalls that display toys and other holiday wares. There are booths with cakes and confections, and others with carvings of Joseph, Mary, and the Magi Kings. There are miniature cows and sheep, asses with long ears and innocent faces, dogs, chickens, and droll little ducks.

The food stalls are as enticing as the toys. The smell of frying potatoes, grilled herring and small pungent sausages fills the air. The boys and girls long for everything they see. Many a hoarded pfennig goes for these delicacies, or for pink sugar-frosted holiday cakes, spiced peppernuts, and *Lebkuchen* — the fancy gingerbreads for which Nuremberg is famous. Children and parents alike joyfully remember Christkindlsmarkt from one year to the next, for here are wonderful sights and smells, and the gold angel that once was the Christ Child doll.

December 24 and January 5
Christmas Eve and Epiphany Eve in Italy

The Pipers' Carol

When the Little Babe
Was born at Bethlehem
It was night,
But the sky was light as day.
Never had stars so brightly shone;
Never had they looked like that.
And the brightest star of all
Went away to call the Kings
From the Orient.

This is the carol of the *zampognari*, or itinerant pipers, who come down from the mountains of Sicily or of Calabria and the Abruzzi at Christmas time. The men pipe pastoral hymns in honor of *Bambino Gesù,* the Baby Jesus. They stop at village shrines and go from house to house to play before the *presepi,* the little homemade Bethlehems, that most families prepare nine days before Christmas.

In these charming manger scenes — which correspond to the French crèche — a pink-cheeked clay or wooden Bambino smiles from his tiny, straw-filled crib. About him are figures of Mary and Joseph, the shepherds and their lambs, the Wise Men with their camels and rich gifts. Sometimes the scenes are costly and elaborate. Often they are a simple family effort in which everyone, from the youngest child to the aged grandparent, has some definite share. The settings are realistic, with bits of stone, moss, and twig for the stable and carved or whittled figures for the Nativity group. Familiar village characters often appear: the old peasant woman with a basket of eggs for the Baby's breakfast; the farmer with a cabbage head; the faggot gatherer with a bundle of sticks to warm the Holy Family. The Bethlehem mangers are precious family heirlooms. Families hand them down and add to them from one generation to another. Frequently everyone gathers before the presepio on each of the nine days preceding Christmas to light candles and offer prayers. Many think that Saint Francis of Assisi, who lived over seven hundred years ago, originated the custom of making the Bethlehems.

Christmas Eve is strictly a family affair. Supper and a party follow attendance at Midnight Mass. Christmas Day is set aside for church and visiting quietly at home. *La Vigilia dell' Epifania,* Epiphany Eve, on January 5, is the time when boys and girls receive presents.

The gift-bearer is *la Befana.* She is the little old witch woman who was sweeping her house on the night when the Wise Men came by with presents for Bambino Gesù. The Kings asked the old woman to go with them to Bethlehem, but she said she must get on with her work. The Kings continued their journey without her. Later, when the sweeping was done, la Befana shouldered her broom and set out for Bethlehem alone. Somehow she lost her way. She has never found the Bambino, although she has searched for almost two thousand years.

Every year la Befana goes through Italy looking for Bethlehem. On her way she always leaves presents for good children. Some people say she does this in memory of the Bambino. Others think she is afraid she may miss Him, and so leaves something for each child.

Italian boys and girls always know when to expect la Befana, just as American children know when Santa Claus is coming. They write letters to ask her for the things they want. The nimble old woman slides down chimneys on her broom handle. She always leaves confections and toys in the shoes or stockings of children who mind their parents, say their prayers, and are not quarrelsome or mean. For the ones who are lazy or rude, she leaves pebbles, lumps of charcoal, or little bags of ash.

December 24 and 25
Christmas Eve and Christmas Day
in Catalonia, Spain

That Great Hour

As that Great Hour
Drew near
When Jesus Christ
Was born,
The trees leafed forth
With green,
And flowers burst
Into bloom,
To glorify His birth.

In Spain, as in many other countries, there is an old folk tradition that trees become green and flowers bloom at midnight on Christmas Eve in honor of the Christ Child.

Christmas Eve in Spain is called *Nochebuena,* the Good Night.
This is the Good Night,
And so is not meant for sleep,
is a popular saying that illustrates the easy Latin grace with which Spanish people combine fairs and Nativity dramas, Midnight Mass and street dancing, in celebration of Jesus' birth.

Almost every town and village has an elaborate Christmas Eve fair. There are toys and *marzipan,* flowers, fruits, vegetables, ducks, and small figures of wood or plaster for the *nacimentos,* or Nativity scenes.

At twelve o'clock the pealing of church bells summons worshippers to Midnight Mass. Richly robed clergy perform the *Misa del Gallo,* or Cock Crow Mass, to the accompaniment of hymns and chants by choir boys and priests. Sometimes Nativity plays form a part of the religious ceremonies. At the Monastery of Montserrat, in Catalonia, magnificent processions, Gregorian chants, and medieval carols glorify the Good Night.

In some cities merrymakers dance in the streets and sing from Midnight Mass until dawn. Christmas Day, following services at the church, is a time of feasting and gaiety. City people receive calls and cards from everyone who has served them during the past year, as well as those who hope for patronage in the year to come. The washerwoman, the garbage collector, the bootblack, and the window cleaner present their greetings of "Merry Christmas and Happy New Year." In return for their good wishes the patron gives each caller a gift of money.

Among the most exciting features of Christmas — as of any feast day in Spain — are parades of the *gigantes*. The gigantes are immense figures made of wood or cardboard. A figure that may measure twenty or thirty feet in height rests on the shoulders of a man hidden inside. A small peephole provides air and allows the performer to see where he is going. The gigantes represent kings, queens, historical, or mythological figures. They dance, jig and whirl to the lively music of the fife and drum. A pair of gypsies usually accompanies the figures and collects Christmas contributions from the spectators.

December 24 and 25
Christmas Eve and Christmas Day
in the Minho, Portugal

O, My Lovely Child

O, my lovely Child,
O, my beautiful Child,
Come, come at once to the world
Because I await your coming.

O, my lovely Child,
O, my beloved Jesus,
Come and save our souls,
And bring Light to the world.

O, My Little One

O, my Child so pretty,
Come, come at once to the world
To save us from captivity,
From the deep abyss.

O, my Child so lovely,
God of infinite beauty,
Come, come at once
And make the hard world soft.

Come everyone, come everyone,
To the stable at Bethlehem.
Worship the Infant Jesus
Who was born for us.

These two beautiful Christmas carols come from the Minho,

Portugal's most northern seacoast province, where the Portuguese nation was born in the twelfth century. People of this ancient province are poor. Although bread is scarce and work hard, peasants of the region love to dance and sing. They wear enchanting costumes and raise great golden-brown oxen with spreading lyre-shaped horns. They make painted pink clay cocks and flower-sprigged clay chickens and celebrate festas every day of the year.

On the night before the Birth of Jesus, bands of carolers go through the streets singing simple songs that tell of the Child who came to earth with Light for men.

Dia da Familia, the Day of the Family, as Christmas is called, is a family festival which as many relatives as possible attend.

In some places the *cepo do Natal,* or traditional oak log, burns on the hearth while the family feasts and drinks. As in Provence, peasants preserve the charred remains throughout the year. Whenever disaster threatens or storms rage, they burn a bit of the ash and offer prayers so the house, the family, and the beasts will not be harmed.

December 25
Christmas Day in Cornwall, England

Sunny Bank

As I sat on a sunny bank,
On Christmas Day in the morning,

I spied three ships come sailing by,
On Christmas Day in the morning.

And who should be with those three ships
But Joseph and his fair lady!

O, he did whistle, and she did sing,
On Christmas Day in the morning.

And all the bells on earth did ring,
On Christmas Day in the morning,

For joy that our Saviour he was born
On Christmas Day in the morning.

Carol singing has always been an important part of English Christmas tradition. Many carols — really the popular songs of the Church — have come down through the centuries with little or no change. As in "Sunny Bank," these songs often give exciting "eyewitness" accounts of some incident, real or imagined, in the Nativity story. Usually the narrative is presented so simply and dramatically that the listener seems to share an event of great spiritual significance.

In this ancient carol, which many think originated in Cornwall, three ships approach "on Christmas Day in the morning." At the helm of one are Joseph and Mary. He is an important

English lord, she his lady. The arrival of the small fleet causes great excitement because it brings news of the birth of Jesus.

In Cornwall, where this carol has long been a favorite, villagers used to meet long before the holidays to decide which "curls" or carols to sing. Many of the songs were handed down in manuscript form from generation to generation. They were often discovered after many years, stowed away in a musty chest in the parish church. Frequently a village or county had its own special carols. Many of the singers were illiterate and they memorized only their own parts. Since old-time curl singers treated the carols as madrigals, the most popular selections were those that gave ample opportunity to "show off" the different parts.

Shortly before Christmas, curl singers visited farms and cottages. They gathered in small groups outside the houses. After whispered directions and muffled throat-clearings, the leader chanted the first line. Then the entire group repeated it in chorus — sometimes once, sometimes several times.

After the curl singers had finished, cottagers invited them inside for "Christmas caake" and something to drink. Cornish folk are traditionally hospitable. At Christmas time especially, even the poorest shares whatever he has with his neighbor.

At the village church on Christmas morning, carols took the place of the usual psalms, and the parish clerk always wished the congregation "Happy Christmas" at the end of the service.

December 25
Christmas Day in India

My Gift To Jesus

O, God, this is the birthday
Of Jesus Christ, Thy Son.
The angels sang on His birthday,
The shepherds heard them
And came to see Him.
The Wise Men brought Him gifts.
Had I been in Bethlehem,
I, too, should have come to Him.
Early in the morning.
My love is the gift I should bring.
Please take it, dear Jesus.

India is a little less than half the size of the United States, excluding Alaska and Hawaii. In square miles India is approximately as big as the combined states of Texas, California, New Mexico, Arizona, Colorado, Utah, Oregon, Idaho, and Wyoming. This land has many different races. The people speak many languages and dialects and have many religious beliefs. India's population is more than three hundred and eighty-one million. Eighty-five per cent are Hindus. But Moslems, Christians, Sikhs, Buddhists, Jews, and other groups live side by side with little interference by state or religious leaders.

India's sacred poem, the *Bhagavat-Gītā,* the Song of the Blessed One — possibly written in the first or second century — tells how God accepts the prayers of all worshipers, regardless of their faith:

As all rivers have the same source —
The water underground —
And as they follow different courses

46 Days of Christmas

Through different lands,
So all religions lead to God.
If you worship me in your own way —
With a flower, with incense, or pouring out of water —
Each act — when done with purity and prayer —
Will reach my throne.

Although Christian Indians make up little more than 2 per cent of the many religious groups, Christianity has been active in the country since the sixteenth century. Dominican friars came to Goa, Portuguese India, as early as 1510. About a quarter of a century later, after Franciscan priests had evangelized western India, Pope Paul III made Goa a bishopric. Saint Francis Xavier, the great Jesuit, visited Goa in the mid-sixteenth century and began training native missionaries at the Franciscan college of Santa Fé, later the College of Saint Paul. This institution became the powerful center of all the Jesuit missions in the East. By the early nineteenth century, Goa had lost much of its original religious importance, but the area still remains a stronghold of the Christian faith.

Each nationality and sect celebrates the festival of Christmas in a different way. Some Christian Indians write their own Christmas songs and sing them to the accompaniment of native musical instruments. Often they compose their own prayers, and present plays or pantomimes to illustrate episodes in the Gospel story.

Many Indians have the crèche at Christmas time, others prefer the lighted tree. In some mountainous areas it is possible to obtain evergreen trees. But in the great central plain where rice, millet, and other grains abound, the native Christians make their own trees from materials at hand.

In one mission center, they used a bundle of rice straw that stood six feet tall. They wound the bundle around and around with coils of twisted rice-straw rope and inserted stubby "branches" of the same material between the coils. As the strange object stood in the mission church, they soaked the straw and plastered it with mud. On Christmas morning they inserted green branches into the damp foundation until the artificial tree resembled a fir in shape. The only decorations were candles, colored paper chains, and mica. The church had no lights, so candles were stuck into clay and placed along bench tops and in the windows. No real evergreen could have been more beautiful in Indian eyes than the homemade tree of straw and mud. To the worshipers, the Christmas message radiated from each lighted candle.

December 24 to January 1
Christmas Eve to New Year's Day in Rumania

Who Will Welcome The Star?

Who will welcome the Star?
The Star, gleaming brightly,
With rays shining forth,
At the birth of Jesus
Was destined to shine
Upon earth
Like a sun.

In Rumanian villages one of the most charming holiday sights is the procession of boys with six-pointed revolving star lanterns. The children gather at dusk and go through the streets and along winding lanes. They stop at each door and sing old carols about the star that shone above the stable at Bethlehem.

Their own stars revolve on long poles. A candle fastened inside lights a bright transparency of the Nativity. Colored streamers, gold paper frills, and tinkling bells make the lanterns as individual as they are gay. To each star point the boys fasten bells. These jingle merrily whenever the star is twirled around, and let villagers know that the singers are coming.

"Who will welcome the Star?" chant the boys, stopping in front of a house.

On Christmas Eve every family has a *turté* — a symbolic cake with many layers of dry paper-thin pastry. Pounded walnuts mixed with honey or melted sugar make the filling. The layers of pastry traditionally represent the Christ Child's swaddling clothes.

In some places the turté, which is prepared on December 23, is part of an ancient fertility rite to increase the fruit crop in the coming year. The housewife plunges her hands into the pastry bowl. With her fingers still covered with dough, she follows her husband to the orchard. They stand before each fruit tree in turn. The man lifts his ax and pretends to cut down the tree. "It is useless and will bear no fruit," he says. The wife always pleads for the life of the tree. As she holds up her hands, she says, "When summer comes this tree will have as much fruit on its branches as I now have dough on my fingers!"

From daybreak until dusk on the day before Christmas, boys run through the hamlet shouting, "Good morning to Uncle Eve." Uncle Eve means Christmas Eve. They chant *colinde,* or recitative songs, about Yuletide, the sun, the moon, and the stars. They also sing about the master and mistress of the house, and even mention their faults. The children are not always tactful, but they receive apples, dried fruits, coins, and sweets in return for their greetings.

On the morning of Christmas Eve the village priest, the sacristan, and a boy with a bowl of holy water start parish rounds. The priest dips a bunch of sweet basil twigs into the water. He sprinkles the house, and blesses it. The housewife drops a coin into the bowl, gives the priest a gift of hemp, and invites him to sit down and eat. Then he goes on to the next cottage.

December 26
Saint Stephen's Day in Ireland

The King Of All Birds

The wren, the wren, the king of all birds,
On Saint Stephen's Day was caught in the furze;
Though his body's small, his family's great,
Come out, Mrs. Grady, and give us a treat.

December 26 is the anniversary of Saint Stephen, the first Christian martyr. Ireland, the Isle of Man, and England once practiced cruel sports on this day in memory of Saint Stephen who was stoned to death. Hunting the Wren, or "wrenning," was once one of the most popular pastimes of the day. The boys killed the wrens, laid the bodies on furze branches and went about the neighborhood demanding money contributions. The boys took their small victims from door to door and sang their verse about the wren as the fifes and fiddles played a lively tune. In the last line they always used the name of the mistress of the house and ended their performance with a few dance steps.

How the wren became "king of all birds" and why it suffered a symbolic death each year are explained in two Irish legends.

In one story the birds could not agree who was really king of all birds. They arranged a contest: the bird who flew the highest would be king. All the birds gathered, big and small, and at a signal they started to fly. Before the race began everyone knew that the eagle — because of his great size and powerful wings — could outfly all other birds. A small brown wren decided to outwit the eagle and win the race through strategy and deceit. Unknown to anyone, he hid in the eagle's crest and mounted rapidly into the sky. Just as the eagle was about to claim the victory, out flew the wren. He chirruped to the birds far below that he, the wren, was highest. He was "king of all birds."

The other legend says the wren and his descendents were killed because they betrayed their country. It happened long ago when the Danes occupied Erin. One night the Irish army was ready to surprise the enemy, who slept in a nearby encampment. Just as the men were ready to launch an attack, a wren hopped out on a Danish drum and alerted the enemy.

Hunting the Wren on Saint Stephen's Day was popular until recently. The sport probably originated in pagan times when living creatures were sacrificed at the feast of the winter solstice. Today Ireland has many tender Christmas customs. On December 24 candles glow in every cottage window "to 'light in' the Redeemer's birth." In southern Ireland the farmer's wife places a tall thick candle on the kitchen table. From Christmas Eve through Epiphany, she lights the candle at dusk and snuffs it out at bedtime.

Christmas is a holy day, and Epiphany the season for giving gifts. On Christmas Eve there is the "black fast" of boiled salt cod and potatoes. Following Mass on the next day, the family gathers for such pleasures as orange treats at dinner, old-fashioned games, and storytelling in front of the hearth.

December 31
New Year's Eve in the Netherlands

Rise, Good People

Rise, good people, rise at once,
For the New Year is at hand;
And so I wish each one of you
Blessings, joy and luck.

These are the words the night watchman of Ootmarsum, a sleepy hamlet in eastern Holland, calls out on New Year's Eve. He clumps through the streets at midnight and proclaims the arrival of another year. From time to time he bangs his night stick on the ancient cobbles to emphasize his greeting to fellow citizens.

In port cities like Rotterdam, prolonged shrieks from sirens on the ships in the harbor and loud blasts of factory whistles announce the New Year.

At eight or nine o'clock on New Year's Eve many persons go to church. The minister usually reviews the year's events and holds a brief memorial for parishioners who have died during the year. Members of the royal family are the only persons he ever mentions by name.

Two things are traditional to the church service: reading the Ninetieth Psalm, "Lord thou hast been our dwelling place in all generations," and singing the eighteenth-century hymn, "Hours, Days, Months, Years, Flee Like a Shadow," by the Dutch poet, Rhijnvis Feith.

Grandparents invite the whole family to visit them after the church service. The group is often large since it includes fathers, mothers, children, and grandchildren, as well as nieces, nephews, uncles, granduncles, and many other relatives.

The New Year's Eve family party is lively with games, charades, and other amusements in which both children and adults take part. Supper is served about eleven o'clock. There are all kinds of delicacies, including many varieties of Dutch cakes, cookies, and fancy breads. *Sneeuballen,* or snowballs, are one of the season's many specialties. Sneeuballen are little balls of pastry rich with butter, eggs, and currants. The dough is fried in deep fat, then drained, and rolled in powdered sugar until the cakes look like miniature snowballs.

At midnight when the church bells peal, everyone embraces and exchanges wishes for health and happiness. The head of the house offers a toast to the coming year. The children are sent to bed, but their elders usually continue to celebrate until the early hours.

New Year's Day is spent calling on friends and eating different kinds of traditional cakes and fruit loaves. The boy or girl who is the first to shout, "Happy New Year," when an uncle, aunt, or other close relative enters the room receives a new gulder for his savings bank.

December 31
New Year's Eve in Bulgaria

Happy, Happy New Year

Happy, happy New Year,
Till next year, till eternity.
Corn on the cornstalk,
Grapes in the vineyard,
Yellow grain in the bin,
Red apples in the garden,
Silkworms in the house,
Happiness and health
Until next year.

For days before the New Year starts, Bulgarian housewives bustle about their kitchens, mixing, rolling, cutting and baking hundreds of little cakes called *kolach*. These cakes with holes in the center are a traditional part of the children's New Year's Eve ceremonies.

Shortly after midnight, when the chimes in the old church tower announce the birth of another year, groups of boys start out on neighborhood rounds. They carry long red switches which they decorate with colored paper flowers. The boys knock on farmhouse doors and sing, "Happy, happy New Year." They wish the house happiness, health, and blessings throughout the year.

At the last loud knock, the door flies open and the boys troop into the kitchen where the family is waiting. Then they start the switching ceremony which probably originated in some early purification rite. Beginning with the grandfather or grandmother and ending with the baby, the boys gently beat each member of the faimly with their branches and "switch in" their good wishes for the New Year.

As a reward for their greetings, the singers receive coins which they pocket, and cakes which they thread on their switches. Then, with shouts of joy, they run off to the next farm to win more cakes before dawn comes.

December 31 to January 6
New Year's Eve to Epiphany
in the Minho, Portugal

We Sing About The Kings

We come to sing about the Kings,
With gaiety and joy,
With gaiety and joy.
For the Little God is born,
Son of the Virgin Mary,
Son of the Virgin Mary.

In the Minho, in northwestern Portugal, masked children go around from house to house between New Year's Eve and Epiphany. They chant *janeiras,* ancient "January" songs. The *janeireiros,* as the singers are called, sometimes improvise verses about the householders. When their presents of wine, sausages, or nuts are generous the performers praise them. If the gifts are few, the whole neighborhood hears about it.

Often, as in this song, the greeting consists of simple repetitive phrases that tell of the Christ Child and the Kings of the East. The singers suggest that they come from far away and are tired and hungry.

People believe that since these old songs supposedly bring good luck in the new year, the singers should be rewarded with coppers, dried figs, and seasonal cakes.

In the Minho there are many wise sayings about the first day of the year. Since New Year's Day supposedly reflects the mood of the next twelve months, one should always have a coin in the pocket, something new on the back, and extra food in the larder. Parents urge their children "to mind their manners" and adults try to act as they wish to act throughout the year. This is why Portugal has the proverb, "Never pay a debt on New Year's Day!"

Our Little God

Come everyone, come everyone,
To worship the King of Glory,
To purify your lips,
To kiss our God.

"O, shepherds, what did you see
In lands where you journeyed?"
"We saw the Child at Bethlehem,
So let us sing, 'Alleluia.' "

This song belongs to the Epiphany Church service. The priest lifts the doll that represents "Our Little God." He invites worshipers to come to the altar and kiss the image. "Purify your lips," he chants.

Epiphany, or *Dia de Reis,* the Day of the Kings, is both secular and religious in character. This is the time when people exchange gifts, and family groups visit from house to house.

In some places the callers stand outside the door and beg permission to come in and sing to the Christ Child. The host welcomes his guests. They enter, sing carols and receive cakes and wine before they call at another house.

As in Belgium, France, and other countries, young people receive presents and attend parties on this day. The *bola-rei,* or Cake of the Kings, contains many surprises. The pastry, which is ring-shaped, hides exciting fortunetelling symbols. But this is not all! Inside the cake there is a single dried broad bean. The one who gets the bean receives a gilt crown and becomes the king of the feast. Next year the king "makes the party" for all his playmates. Adults follow much the same custom at their Epiphany parties. Whoever finds the bean pays for the cake in the coming year.

Hallelujah, Gentlemen!

Hallelujah, gentlemen!
Tomorrow's the Day of the Magi Kings,
The greatest feast of Spain.
We ask for holiday presents
In memory of Bethlehem's Child.
We ask for holiday presents
And gifts of good things to eat.

Spanish boys and girls impatiently wait for Epiphany Eve when the Magi Kings, Caspar, Melchior and Balthasar, travel through Spain on their way to Bethlehem. On their journey to the Holy Land the Kings leave presents for children.

Before going to bed, the young people stuff hay or grain into their shoes and leave them on the balcony or near the door for the Wise Men's horses. By morning the food is always gone and in its place are all kinds of festive cakes, candies, and gay playthings of straw or clay.

Parents often blacken the cheeks of sleeping boys and girls with charcoal during the night. In the morning the children hurry to the mirror to see if Balthasar, the Black King, has kissed them in passing.

In many cities in Spain, as in Mallorca and the Canary Islands, Epiphany begins with colorful processions of the Magi Kings and their retinues. At Palma the Kings arrive by torchlight. The city officials lead on horseback. The Kings also ride horses which their servants attend. Last of all come the Magi's retainers, in brilliant oriental robes of yellow, green and red. At Las Palmas, in the Canary Islands, the procession is even more dramatic, since the Kings arrive by camel.

The Hallelujah comes from the province of Burgos, where boys wander through the town on Epiphany Eve. They remind householders that the next day is the Feast of the Magi Kings, and they ask for gifts of food in the Christ Child's name.

January 6
Three Kings' Day in Belgium

Three Kings, Three Kings

Three Kings, Three Kings,
Give me a new hat,
My old one is worn out.
Mother must not know this:
Father counted coins on the grill!

On *Driekonigendag,* or Three Kings' Day, bands of children in grotesque costumes go around from farm to farm. They sing nonsense verses about the Kings and receive gifts of coins and cakes.

The last line of this song refers to the open metal grill that decorates the top of old-fashioned Belgian charcoal braziers. In the song, the father has carelessly counted coins for a new hat on top of the grill. Of course, the money fell through and was lost. Because of this accident the children feel they should have a few extra centimes on Three Kings' Day.

As in many other countries, Three Kings' Day is a party occasion in Belgium. There is always a *gâteau des rois,* or Cake of the Kings. This is no ordinary party cake. As in Portugal, it contains a dried bean and the child who discovers it in his portion receives royal honors for the day.

The King chooses a Queen or, if a girl finds the bean, she names a King. The royal pair receives gold paper crowns and robes that are often pieced together from purple, orange, or scarlet scraps.

The young King and Queen rule the party. Whatever they do the court imitates. Whenever the royal pair laughs, for example, the courtiers shout, "The King laughs! The Queen laughs!" and burst out laughing. When the two sneeze, everyone sneezes; when they dance, everyone dances.

January 6 (Old Style)
Christmas Eve, Armenian Apostolic Church

O, Great And Wondrous Mystery

O, great and wondrous Mystery, revealed to us today!
Shepherds and angels sing,
"A King is born in Bethlehem."
Sing, sons of men, He comes to save you.
Heaven and earth together meet.
Heaven declares joy to both,
Earth wears salvation's robe.
Shepherds see the Light of the World
And with the angels sing,
"Glory to God on High."

Although the Armenian people are now without an independent state, they have an independent church. Saint Gregory, "the Illuminator," founded the Armenian Apostolic Church. Gregory, who was born about 257, was the first bishop of the Church and later its patron saint. Throughout the centuries the Armenian Apostolic Church has given to the world a rich body of devotional literature. Among the many hymns are chants such as "Great and Wondrous Mystery." Armenians, wherever they may be, sing it at Christmas Eve communion.

The Armenian Christmas comes on January 7, in the Old Style calendar. In the Old Style, the dates are thirteen days later than in the Gregorian calendar, which the Western world uses.

Christmas is a great religious festival for which careful preparations are made. The house, like the soul, must be ready to receive the Son of God. The week before Christmas housewives start to scrub and polish. Whenever possible they buy new clothes for the family. If they cannot afford new clothes, they brush and press, wash and mend old ones so everyone will look his best.

More important than these outward preparations are the prayer and repentance that precede the Christmas Eve communion. The fasting of the week means denial of foods such as eggs, milk, butter, animal fats, and meat. On the day of the service everyone, except old people and children, tries to fast from sunrise until after communion.

At the church service, the chant "Christ is born and revealed today" follows each verse of the Christmas hymn. After Saint Luke's story of the manger birth is read and the *Gloria* sung, the communicants kneel at the altar. Following the service everyone hurries home to enjoy the Christmas Eve supper.

The fast is over except for eating meat, which is forbidden until after the Christmas morning service. Fried fish, lettuce, and boiled spinach are among the traditional feast-night foods. Spinach is important, for tradition says that the Virgin Mary ate spinach for supper on the night Jesus was born. In old Armenia people observed the mystic rule of seven, which meant seven fruits, seven nuts, seven other foods, and water drawn from seven wells for the holiday feast.

In old Armenia also, everyone retired early and rose before dawn on Christmas morning. In the country worshipers carried lanterns to light their way across fields and along dark winding roads. At the church myriads of candles burned brightly and the choir announced the glad tidings with the words:

> *Joyfully we celebrate*
> *Thy Holy Birth,*
> *O, Light of Lights,*
> *Who revealed Thyself to Man,*
> *And filled the world*
> *With Thy Light.*

January 18 (Old Style)
Old Twelfth Night, Somerset, England

46 Days of Christmas

Here's To Thee, Old Apple Tree

Here's to thee, old apple tree,
Whence thou may'st bud
And whence thou may'st blow,
And whence thou may'st
Bear apples enow.
Bushel, bushel, sacks full,
And my pockets full, too. Huzza!

Some of England's West Country communities still wassail, or toast, the apple trees on January 18, Old Twelfth Night. In apple-producing regions, wassailing — which comes from the Old English *waes hael,* "be thou hale" — was once a fertility rite. Farmers believed it ensured health and good crops to their fruit trees in the coming year. Today few remember how the custom began, but it continues to be a rousing climax to the holiday festivities.

The wassailing varies from place to place. At Carhampton, in Somerset, villagers light their lanterns at night and make the rounds of the orchards. The group carries a large pail of cider with a piece of toast floating on top. One man has a gun.

The wassailers circle one of the most vigorous trees. They place the toast in a crotch "for the robins." The toast keeps birds from bud-nipping, farmers say; but in ancient times, they probably regarded both the toast and the cider as offerings to the vegetation spirit that guarded the tree.

The men crowd close to the tree. The leader pours cider around the roots.

The villagers sing:

"To your wassail and my wassail
And joy be to our jolly wassail."

The man with the gun fires through the upper branches, "to scare away evil spirits." Everyone drinks a mug of cider to the health of the orchard. Before the night ends, the group holds a similar ceremony before many apple trees. This is probably why Somerset farmers boast that their fruit crops are the heaviest and their cider the best in the world.

INDEX BY COUNTRY

ALPHABETICAL INDEX OF TITLES

INDEX BY SPECIAL DAYS